Yona Zeldis McDonough

LOUISA
THE LIFE OF
LOUISA MAY ALCOTT

ILLUSTRATED BY

Bethanne Andersen

Christy Ottaviano Books
HENRY HOLT AND COMPANY
NEW YORK

Henry Holt and Company, LLC, *Publishers since 1866*
175 Fifth Avenue, New York, New York 10010
www.HenryHoltKids.com

Henry Holt® is a registered trademark of Henry Holt and Company, LLC.
Text copyright © 2009 by Yona Zeldis McDonough
Illustrations copyright © 2009 by Bethanne Andersen
Distributed in Canada by H. B. Fenn and Company Ltd.

Library of Congress Cataloging-in-Publication Data
McDonough, Yona Zeldis.
Louisa: the life of Louisa May Alcott / Yona Zeldis McDonough ;
illustrated by Bethanne Andersen.—1st ed.
p.   cm.
"Christy Ottaviano Books."
Includes bibliographical references.
ISBN-13: 978-0-8050-8192-3 / ISBN-10: 0-8050-8192-5
1. Alcott, Louisa May, 1832–1888—Juvenile literature. 2. Authors, American—
19th century—Biography—Juvenile literature. I. Andersen, Bethanne, ill. II. Title.
PS1018.M347 2009   813'.4—dc22   2008038222

First Edition—2009 / Designed by April Ward
Printed in October 2010 in the United States of America by Lehigh Phoenix,
Rockaway, New Jersey, on acid free paper ∞

3 5 7 9 10 8 6 4 2

The artist used gouache and pastel on Arches buff paper
to create the illustrations for this book.

For Kate, my eager reader
—Y. Z. M.

For Gail, Louanne, and
Collen, who made being
little women an art
—B. A.

ON A COLD, blustery day in 1832, a baby girl—the second in the Alcott family—was born. Her parents, Bronson and Abigail, named her Louisa May. She already had a big sister, Anna, and soon two more sisters, Elizabeth and May, joined her.

Bronson taught school in Germantown, Pennsylvania. He had very unusual ideas for his time. He believed both boys and girls should be educated and that their opinions were important. He thought that children should be given the same respect as adults.

Bronson's ideas were
considered unconventional
and even strange. People began
to take their children out of
his school, and it soon closed.

The Alcotts moved to
Boston, where Bronson found
a new job. Boston was a busy,
exciting place. Louisa liked
exploring, which sometimes
got her into trouble. When
she was six, she took a walk
all by herself. It grew dark,
and Louisa became lost. But
she didn't cry. Instead, she
sat down, put her head on the
back of a big friendly dog, and
fell asleep. Later, her worried
parents came to get her.

Another time, she was walking on Boston Common with her mother. The Common was a large grassy area, like a park. When her mother turned away for a minute, Louisa fell into the frog pond. A kind black boy jumped in and pulled her out. He ran away before anyone could thank him, but Louisa always remembered him.

This was a period when slavery still existed in America. Louisa's parents were abolitionists, people who believed slavery was wrong and should be ended. Around this time, Bronson invited a young black girl to attend the school where he was teaching. Again, his unconventional views angered parents, and they withdrew their children. The school closed, and Bronson had to find another job. The family packed up and moved to Concord, Massachusetts.

Louisa soon loved her new home. The house was small, but there were gardens, fields, woods, and a river for her to explore. Life in Concord was filled with so many good things that Louisa didn't realize how poor her family now was. Her father took jobs chopping wood, gardening, or helping out a neighboring farmer.

Bronson was an idealistic man, though not too practical. Louisa's mother loved him, but she was always worried about money. She worked hard at chores and housework. Even when Bronson earned money, he felt compelled to give much of it away to people who were worse off than his family.

Still, the Alcotts had good times, like the pillow fights Bronson started every Saturday night. They all joined in, swinging pillows and laughing until Bronson conceded that, yes, the girls had won.

The girls gave strawberry
parties out in the woods
and wrote plays, which they
acted out. Using scraps from
Abigail's ragbag, Louisa made
fabulous costumes for her
sisters. These were some of the
happiest times in Louisa's life.

Louisa, like her sisters, went to school in Concord. She didn't much care for arithmetic or grammar, but loved reading, writing, history, and geography. And sometimes she felt that nature was her best subject of all. The hills, meadows, trees, and flowers taught her what no books could teach. She described running through the woods on a fall morning and stopping to watch the sun rise. "A very strange and solemn feeling came over me as I stood there," she later wrote in her journal, "with no sound but the rustle of the pines, no one near me, and the sun so glorious, as for me alone. It seemed as if I *felt* God as I never did before, and I prayed in my heart that I might keep that happy sense of nearness in my life."

It was in Concord that Louisa first started writing poems and stories. Her mother, wanting to encourage her, gave Louisa a pencil case for her tenth birthday. Urged by their parents, all the Alcott girls kept journals. Louisa filled hers with observations about herself, her family, and the life that was unfolding around her.

Louisa began to understand her family's financial situation and grew worried. Once she tried to earn money as a doll's dressmaker. She chased the neighbor's hens for their feathers and made fancy dolls' hats to sell. When her shoes became too tight, she went bare-foot instead of telling her mother since there was no money for a new pair. She started thinking about her future and what she wanted to be when she grew up.

Actress? Artist? Writer? Whatever it was, she vowed that she would make enough money to support the people she loved. "I *will* do something by and by," she wrote. "Don't care what: teach, sew, act, write, anything to help the family."

In the spring of 1842, Bronson was invited to England to share his alternative ideas about education. Although he was too poor to afford the trip, his good friend, the writer Ralph Waldo Emerson, got him the money he needed. When Bronson returned, he was filled with enthusiasm for a new plan. He moved his family to a communal farm called Fruitlands. The plan was to work the land together with some of their friends and create a model world.

Things went well at first, but then winter came. Several people decided life at Fruitlands was too hard and left. One woman was asked to leave because she ate fish. (The members of the community were vegetarians and did not eat meat, chicken, or fish.) The few who stayed were unable to continue; the weather was harsh, and food was in short supply. The grand experiment failed, leaving Bronson bitterly disappointed. He became seriously ill, and Louisa's mother nursed him back to health.

When Bronson was well enough, the family moved back to Concord. But then Abigail Alcott was offered a job with the South End Friendly Society in Boston, and she decided that she must accept it. So the Alcotts packed their things and moved yet another time.

At seventeen, Louisa was now old enough to work. She taught school and looked after young children. She sewed and did chores for other people. Once, Louisa was offered a job to do light housework and read aloud to a woman who was ill. But when she got there, she was expected to do hard work, like carrying coal and water, scrubbing, shoveling snow, and cutting firewood—and no reading. Louisa was furious at being lied to and left the job after a month. All that she was paid for her weeks of labor was four dollars. She was so angry she sent back the money.

But Louisa's writing had begun to get noticed. One of her stories was published in a magazine, and she was paid five dollars. In 1854, when Louisa was twenty-two, a publisher brought out a collection of her stories. It was called *Flower Fables* and it earned her thirty-two dollars. When the book appeared, she tucked it into her mother's stocking on Christmas morning.

As much as Louisa loved to
write, she couldn't earn a living
from doing it. She made a little
money from selling more stories
and a little more from sewing.
While she sewed, she created
new stories in her head and later
wrote them down.

Louisa was able to find work
teaching, though she didn't much
like it. She was very homesick
and missed her family. It was
during this time that her sister
Elizabeth, who had long been
frail, grew sick and died of
scarlet fever. Louisa had come
home at the end and was there
to hold her sister's hand and
kiss her good-bye. The whole
family grieved terribly over
Elizabeth's death.

Following the funeral, Louisa went back to Boston. She continued her teaching and writing, occasionally publishing stories in various magazines and working on a novel. She returned home to care for her mother when she got sick and to attend Anna's wedding to John Pratt. Then, in 1862, Louisa made a startling decision: She would go to Washington as a nurse.

The Civil War had broken out the year before, and the Northern armies were fighting the Southern states in a bitter struggle over slavery. Louisa had always been opposed to slavery; here was a chance to put her beliefs into action. "I became an Abolitionist at a very early age," she wrote. She conjectured it might have been because "I was saved from drowning in the Frog Pond . . . by a colored boy."

Louisa arrived in Washington late one December evening. The hospital had once been a hotel but was now filled with cots, blankets, and all sorts of medical supplies. Her own room was a bare chamber shared with two other nurses. Many of the windows were broken, and she heard the scratching of rats in the closet. But she didn't let any of that bother her.

She rose at six every day, dressed by gaslight, and went quickly through the ward, opening windows to let in the fresh air.

Louisa spent the morning giving out rations, cutting up food, sweeping, making beds, dressing wounds, and sewing bandages. After lunch, soldiers dictated letters they wanted to send. It was a hard life, but she wrote, "Though often homesick, heartsick, and worn out, I like it—find real pleasure in comforting, tending, and cheering these poor souls."

After a month, Louisa came down with typhoid fever. Her father had to bring her home. Later, she wrote, "My greatest pride is in the fact that I lived to know the brave men and women who did so much for the cause, and that I had a very small share in the war which put an end to a great wrong."

It took Louisa many months to recover, and when she did she began writing what she called "Hospital Sketches." First published in a newspaper, the sketches were very popular, and two publishers asked if they could bring out a collection of them in book form. The finished book was a success. She was able to publish the novel she had been working on, *Moods*, in 1864, and then had a chance to visit Europe as a paid companion to a woman who was ill.

When she returned, a publisher asked if she could write a "girls' book." She said she would try. The result was *Little Women*, published in 1868. Louisa didn't feel too hopeful about her latest work. "Never liked girls or knew many, except my sisters; but our queer plays and experiences may prove interesting, though I doubt it."

Louisa had never been more mistaken in her life. Girls adored the story of the four March sisters and their beloved Marmee. Louisa used many of the experiences from her own early life in the book: the house in Concord, the money worries, the plays, and the games. Jo, the tomboy with literary ambitions, was modeled after Louisa herself. Beth, the gentle, sweet sister who died young, was based on Elizabeth. The model for Amy was May. Laurie was actually a combination of two different people: Ladislas Wisniewski, a Polish boy she had met in Europe, and Alf Whitman, a good and loyal friend. Aunt March was loosely based on Louisa's own generous but strict great-aunt Hancock.

The publisher was so happy with the reaction to *Little Women*, he asked for more. A second volume quickly followed, and it was even more popular than the first. (Today, both volumes appear in a single book.) Louisa was a great success now. Reporters came to interview her, and strangers often stopped her in the street. She was happy that so many people were reading her work, but she didn't like giving up her privacy. And her health was not good. Although she didn't know it, the medicine she had taken when she was sick in Washington contained mercury. The mercury stayed in her body and was slowly poisoning her. Still, she kept writing and publishing books.

The money she made allowed her to travel, something she really enjoyed. She went to Europe again, with her sister May and May's friend Alice Bartlett. They had a wonderful time in France, in an old town called Dinan. The letters they wrote home described their adventures: exploring ruined castles, being chased by angry pigs, riding in a donkey cart with a driver who had had too much to drink, eating so much of the delicious local food that they became "fat and hearty."

Louisa also visited New York City, where she spent time at hospitals, orphanages, and asylums. She was always interested in people who were poor. She must have understood how they suffered.

Her beloved mother was growing feeble and, in 1877, passed away. Louisa took solace in knowing she had made the last years of her mother's life comfortable and free from financial worry. Her sister May had married a man named Ernest Nieriker. Soon, the couple had a little girl, whom they named Louisa May. When tragically May died shortly after the birth, little Lulu went to live with Louisa, in accordance with May's last wishes.

Louisa remained utterly devoted to what was left of her family and spent her life taking care of them. She was now able to afford expensive silk dresses, and she had homes both in Concord and on Beacon Hill—a refined Boston neighborhood—which she divided her time between.

Her last novel, *Jo's Boys*, was a sequel to *Little Women*, and Lulu's Library was three books of stories written especially for Lulu. But by now, Louisa's ill health prevented her from doing much work.

One day in early March 1888, she went to see her ailing father. She thought it might be the last time she saw him. During their visit, she found him "very sweet and feeble." He must have known that he was dying, for he said to her, "I am going up. Come with me."

On her way home, she was so upset that she forgot to wear her warm cloak and caught a bad chill. The next day, she had a terrible headache and soon fell unconscious with pneumonia. She lingered briefly before peacefully dying. After Louisa's death, Lulu went to Germany, where she was raised by her father.

Louisa May Alcott was only fifty-five when she died, but she had lived a rich, full life, both in the world and in the pages of her wonderful books, which children and adults continue to read—and love—today.

THE WORLD ACCORDING TO LOUISA MAY ALCOTT

On her childhood: "Our poor little home had much love and happiness in it, and was a shelter for lost girls, abused wives, friendless children, and weak or wicked men."

On nature: "I ran in the wind . . . and had a lovely time in the woods with Anna and Lizzie. We were fairies, and made gowns and paper wings. I 'flied' the highest of all."

On work: "Won't go home to sit idle while I have a head and a pair of hands."

"Work is and has always been my salvation."

"Housekeeping ain't no joke."

On being a nurse during the Civil War: "I hope . . . that the Washington experience may do me lasting good. To go very near to death teaches one to value life, and this winter will always be a very memorable one to me."

On poverty: "Hate to visit people who ask me to help amuse others, and often longed for a crust in a garret with freedom and a pen."

On money: "I love luxury, but freedom and independence better."

On fame: "People *must* learn that authors have some rights; I can't entertain a dozen a day, and write the tales they demand also."

On her niece Lulu: "My heart is full of pride and joy, and the touch of the dear little hands seems to take away the bitterness of grief. I often go in at night to see if she is really *here*, and the sight of the little head is like sunshine to me."

On her poor health: "It is tiresome to be always aching. Why can't people use their brains without breaking down?"

On growing older: "The wheel of fortune turned slowly, till the girl of fifteen found herself a woman of fifty, with her prophetic dream beautifully realized, her duty done, her reward far greater than she deserved."

"Hearts don't grow old."

LOUISA THE POET

Louisa loved writing poetry. Here is one
of her earliest poems, written in 1840, when
she was only eight years old:

To the First Robin

Welcome, welcome, little stranger,
Fear no harm, and fear no danger;
We are glad to see you here,
For you sing "Sweet Spring is near."

Now the white snow melts away;
Now the flowers blossom gay:
Come dear bird and build your nest,
For we love our robin best.

This poem was written a little later, in 1843, when she was eleven:

To Mother

I hope that soon, dear mother,
You and I may be
In the quiet room my fancy
Has so often made for thee,—

The pleasant, sunny chamber,
The cushioned easy-chair,
The book laid for your reading,
The vase of flowers so fair;

The desk beside the window
Where the sun shines warm and bright:
And there in ease and quiet
The promised book you write;

While I sit close beside you,
Content at last to see
That you can rest, dear mother,
And I can cherish thee.

Interesting Facts About Louisa May Alcott, Her Writing, and Her Family

There have been at least six movie versions made of *Little Women*. Some of the actresses who played in these movies were Katharine Hepburn (1933), Elizabeth Taylor (1949), Winona Ryder (1994), and Claire Danes (1994).

The Alcotts followed the dietary rules of Sylvester Graham (he created the graham cracker) and didn't eat sugar, meat, or butter. They didn't drink coffee or tea either. The Alcotts believed in sleeping on hard mattresses, taking cold baths, and getting lots of fresh air.

The members of Fruitlands did not wear cotton because cotton had been picked by slaves. Nor did they wear wool because it had been made from the fleece of animals. Instead, they made clothing from linen, a cloth made from the flax plant.

Lulu Nieriker, Louisa's niece, died in 1975, at the age of ninety-six. Lulu had one daughter, six grandchildren, and six great-grandchildren.

Orchard House, where Louisa once lived, is now a museum. Each year, about 55,000 people visit the house, which is in Concord, Massachusetts.

New England Apple Slump

Louisa May Alcott was so fond of this traditional New England dessert that she called her Concord, Massachusetts, house Apple Slump. Here is a recipe for that dessert.

Ingredients

6 tart apples, peeled, cored, and sliced
½ cup brown sugar
¼ teaspoon nutmeg
¼ teaspoon cinnamon
¼ teaspoon salt

Topping

1½ cups flour
2 teaspoons double-acting baking powder
½ teaspoon salt
½ cup sugar
1 egg, beaten
½ cup milk
1 stick (½ cup) unsalted butter, melted and cooled
cream for whipping (optional)

Directions

Toss apples with brown sugar, spices, and salt. Place in a buttered baking dish and bake at 350°F for 20 minutes.

Topping: Sift together flour, baking powder, and salt. In a separate bowl, mix remaining ingredients. Add to dry ingredients, stirring till just combined. Spread topping over apples, and bake at 350°F for 25 minutes. Top with whipped cream if desired.

IMPORTANT DATES IN THE
LIFE OF LOUISA MAY ALCOTT

March 16, 1831   Sister Anna Bronson Alcott is born in Germantown

November 29, 1832   Louisa May Alcott is born in Germantown

March 16, 1834   The Alcotts move to Boston

June 24, 1835   Sister Elizabeth Sewall Alcott is born in Boston

July 26, 1840   Sister Abba May Alcott is born in Concord

June 1, 1843   The Alcotts move to Fruitlands in Harvard

April 1, 1845   The Alcotts move to Concord

1855   Louisa goes off to Boston alone to try to earn money

March 14, 1858   Elizabeth Alcott dies

December 13, 1862   Louisa becomes a nurse in the Civil War

August 1863   *Hospital Sketches* is published

October 1, 1868   Part One of *Little Women* is published

April 14, 1869   Part Two *of Little Women* is published

April 1870   *An Old-Fashioned Girl* is published

June 1871   *Little Men* is published in America

September 25, 1875   *Eight Cousins* is published

November 1876   *Rose in Bloom* is published

November 25, 1877   Louisa's mother dies

March 22, 1878   Abba May marries Ernest Nieriker

October 15, 1878   *Under the Lilacs* is published

November 8, 1879   Louisa's niece Louisa May Nieriker (called Lulu) is born

December 29, 1879   Abba May dies

September 19, 1880   Lulu comes to live with Louisa in Boston

October 9, 1880   *Jack and Jill* is published

October 9, 1886   *Jo's Boys* is published in America

March 4, 1888   Louisa's father dies

March 6, 1888   Louisa dies in Boston

BIBLIOGRAPHY

Graves, Kerry A., ed. *The Girlhood Diary of Louisa May Alcott, 1843–1846*. Mankato, MN.: Blue Earth Books, 2001.

Greene, Carol. *Louisa May Alcott: Author, Nurse, Suffragette*. Chicago: Children's Press, 1984.

Ruth, Amy. *Louisa May Alcott*. Minneapolis: Lerner Publications, 1999.

Ryan, Cary, ed. *Louisa May Alcott: Her Girlhood Diary*. Mahwah, NJ: Bridgewater Books, 1993.

Santrey, Laurence. *Louisa May Alcott: Young Writer*. Mahwah, NJ: Troll Associates, 1986.

Silverthorne, Elizabeth. *Louisa May Alcott*. Philadelphia: Chelsea House Publishers, 2002.